Mothers Lovers & Others

new and selected poems

by Raven

Mothers Lovers & Others

new and selected poems

by Raven

TSEpress

MOTHERS, LOVERS & OTHERS
new and selected poems by Raven

Cover Design and Interior & Layout Design: MyPublishedBook.com
Cover Photo: Raven

ISBN 979-8-218-52939-0 (paperback)

for Julia

Table of Contents

M O T H E R S

L O V E R S

OTHERS

Mothers

Generations

This new seed cradled in blood and bone
starts with a pull in the womb
seed
root
struggling shoot
emerges from this fertile shelter
destined to seek a separate journey

she leaves behind a memory
absorbed by my bones and blood.

bones, that grieve the leaching of marrow
learn the weight of loss
wrap and cradle
my tender heart

blood, moon's messenger
recalling lunar cycles waxing and waning
reminding me of the
relentless rightness of tides

Across time
I hear the echo of blood, bone and memory
calling again to give away
small pieces of my heart
creating empty spaces
frayed with longing.
I am a willing donor.

In a miracle not of science but of love
these chambers mend renewed in wholeness
bearing witness to the convergence of heart and memory
in harmony with the future.

Mother

Inky spill of
anchoring womb
root and stem that twist and tangle
Entangle me.

Catch and clutch
my slender green reeds
that struggle and survive
Release me.

Earth

Earth is the womb from
which we emerge
claiming our spirit in
vibrant connection with her

we are born within her ancient knowing
remembering the answer to the only question
of who we must become
before she calls us back.

Water

We are water
silent and eternal
beginning as a single drop
formed in the thermal melt of a glacier
tumbling forward converging in
stream
river
ocean
mindful of harnessing our gathering power
proclaiming a sacred hymn of renewal
our saltwater blessing

Portrait

Squeezed straight from the painter's tube
myth and mystery
fuse in a palette of colors

primary
primal

I am the blood-red of Lucretia
electric blue of a dime-store plastic virgin
yellow that scorches like a solar flare

I am a bold black raven a
glint of silver held in my mouth and
just as fearless

Avocado

It's the pit that counts
not the smooth green-goddess pulp
so pretty to look at so
pleasing to our tongue.

Stabilizing all that surrounds it, the
pit slips out sometimes unnoticed
frequently discarded. A solid core that
holds the life seed and nutrients
needed for the possibility of future growth.

cherish that center
reconsider its value
don't be so quick to toss it aside

You may one day be a Mother, too.

Bella Collina

Pale hydrangeas stand tall with
sturdy stems
burgeoning leaves
unyielding like stalwart sentries

their scent rises up
past weathered railings splintered with age
above stone staircases worn centuries smooth
joining soft breezes like ancient perfume
lingering over the still blue-gray sea.

On coarse sand where
time-worn mountains meet timeless tides
I recall my venerable origins
in the curve of the bay and
faint but familiar language
buried in my heart.

This DNA has left me stranded
so far from home.

Yielding to memories
I am drawn back now to
stone staircases
well-trodden paths and
sweetly scented hydrangeas.

When I Was 12 Years Old

When I was 12
my world blew apart and
landed up-side-down.
My sister was born
sticky with need and
my family came unglued.

Cartographer/Cryptographer

A daughter, like the God Janus,
can face the past with you but
must look to the future alone.

She learns to navigate the dance
like Ginger Rogers
nimble both backward and forward.

She needs your Cartographer skills
to map the origins of her past in
tandem with yours.

But she trains as a Cryptographer
solving secrets of the past
while writing new code for the future.

Abuela

Your face is a sewing lesson
creased
draped
pinch-pleated
lined
patterned with age.

My hand-stitched memory.

Needle and Thread

My Grandmother knew her way around
a needle and thread her
wrist pin cushion a constant companion
she stitched hems and cuffs
collars and seams.

In the gentle piercing and pulling of threads
she somehow bound us all together
silently taking our measure
stitching us piece by piece
to each other.

My family would scatter like loose buttons in a tin
only to be caught up again, whole-cloth
in her capable hands
patched, mended, rejoined in love.

Pattern Maker

She gathered friends
like she gathered fabric scraps
a few from her Grandmother's day
soft and flanneled

Some from long afternoons
spent with her mother
faded and worn

Some from her children's playmates
flashy and vibrant

Faded or flashy, worn or vibrant
they were patterned with memories
each with a story to tell

She wove these stories of youth labor suffering joy
together in a harmonious tapestry
her friendships a patchwork crazy quilt of
multigenerational love

I am a fraying rope
twisted strands of past and present
woven taut and strong
now drying and brittle with age

Each unraveling a surprise

Letting Go

Thin aged cicada
forced to surrender her voice.
Winter has arrived.

Be Still

I never knew how to live by being still
I fidgeted
spoke up
    talked fast
           raced forward
reached
      high
laughed
      TOO LOUDLY
sped through days and weeks
and years

Now I am learning stillness
slowing my pace
valuing the occasional
Full Stop.

Lovers

Somewhere someone needs love.
Everywhere everyone needs love.

So spool out a gossamer thread from deep in your heart
wrap it around the whole earth
over
    and
        under
criss-crossing rivers and oceans
mountains and shorelines
until we are all bundled in tenderness

then weave one more silvery path
through the noise and night
directly to my waiting heart and
stitch your luminous light to mine.

Sweet and Salt

The freshwater baptism
that is the sweet of you
the barely perceptible rise and fall
of your breath when you are sleeping
your slowly awakening wonder
in the early morning
your reach for me
your honey-blossom kisses
whispers like a Nightingale's song.

You are my morning coffee
my Belgian chocolate
candy held in my mouth to make it last.

You are a rare spice
precious salt traded by Kings and Emperors
lending your buoyancy to the sea
I taste it in your tears and
on your freckled shoulder
it sings on my lips
stings in your careless words.

I slip into the liminal space where
the sweet and the salt join and
meet you there.

Reflection

Your body holds weightless moonlight
diffused through torso and limb
head and heart
spilling out from
mouth and eyes
reflected onto my body.

Your light mixes with stardust magic
making me think it is my own
no card tricks
no rabbit in a top hat
no sleight of hand

just the generosity of love.

Early Morning in February

I rest my cheek close to yours
while you are sleeping still
warm whispery breath brushes my face a
slow rhythmic pulse like music heard in small spaces.

I lay my head on your chest
hear the echo of your inhale and exhale
rise and fall in harmony with the
steady beat of your heart.

Held tenderly in breath and beat
my own heart rests.

Whew!

Early morning
my body stilled briefly by sleep paralysis
mouth dry as cobwebs
limbs heavy as river clay
I resist the pull to leave night behind
where my skin is flushed with heat
my face reddened in a
blush of private reverie

Oh, I need to take a moment!

to hold on to the ghost of you
savor the lingering weight and warmth of you
before knowing for certain
it was only a dream

Fire

Fire is a dance that moves between us
illuminating our spirit
reaching for Eden
again and again

fire lives beyond the
fullness of touch
fades early
denies its own return

fire
whose ultimate fate is
vapor and ash

Wild Flower Kisses

I dream the warm buzzy tingle of your kiss
floral fragrance of spicy frangipani
honeysuckle taste as sweet as sunlight
lips like morning dew.
Promises of jasmine for love
freesia for trust
prevail over the tease of lupines
hinting at risk.

I dream a meadow.
It is you.

A hesitant gesture
full of uncertainty
you lean in to kiss me the
buzz of your lips brushes mine
with an unexpected   tingle

that grows to a   tickle

that triggers a   giggle

that burbles into a   gulp!

a wild Zing! of hiccuping laughter
that spills out
spoiling the moment.

Sorry.

Be Safe. Keep Cover Closed.

My matchbook heart
flipped open by your crooked smile
ignited by your careless fingers
left spent and exposed.

Better to be safe. Keep cover closed.

Old Blue Eyes

Your eyes
as deep as an inky spill
wash over me like a frigid winter wave
as hard as river stones in early morning light
they leave me cold

blue as a tear and half in love with loneliness

Object Permanence

In my dreams last night my car was towed
parked illegally, I knew it could happen but
I was in careless denial

I always expect some things or some one should be
precisely where I need them to be.
My belief keeps the universe spinning on its axis

until it doesn't

In fact, my car was hooked two wheels up
jolting its way down main street and
when I reached for you in the morning

you were gone

Air

we believe in what we cannot see

a song in the wind

a whisper

a giggle

a secret

each memory a breath

I'll never get over my love of laughter.

There's baby's first gurgle that burbles with glee
polite tee-hee behind a shy hand
low throaty heh-heh with its subtle eye-wink.

There's the belly-shaker sillier than you think
explosive milk-coming-out-of-your-nose snort
deafening roar that jumps to its feet at the first score.

Then there is your singular laugh
a sort of gulping
 gasping
    st- ut-ter- y
 hah-
      hah
that gains speed and builds to a merry crescendo

its sound like music in my heart.

Animé

It's invisible
but try living without one.

You can search it or bare it.
It can be deep or old or
sold to an unscrupulous buyer.

It can be a spiritual connection
to a sister or brother or mate
kinship chosen not assigned.

Often it's paired with body or heart
as if it needs a companion to be complete.

It has its signature food to nourish us
music that moves us.

They say confession is good for it
but that's not my experience.

I know only this for certain
when I am with you
my soul like a tiny toy mouse
squeaks and squeals with joy.

A Good Listener

I once had a lover who punctuated every sentence
with an emphatic
Right? Am I right?

Was he really asking
for agreement
affirmation
support or
confirmation?

What if I didn't agree?
If his thinking was flawed
his claims misguided
if I couldn't confirm
with a nod?

I couldn't answer
what I thought he was really asking
Do you love me? Do you love me?

Luna Meets Neil Armstrong

My untouched skin trembles
brushed by a plume of powdery dust as

he settles onto my cold dry folds
I open to the weight of his body
in wordless surprise

embrace the mystery of his presence
knowing I want to be his only

Moon mistress.

Sunday Morning Radio

Wait! Wait! Don't tell me.
That's what I want to shout.

Don't tell me that you are leaving and
taking the cat with you.

Don't tell me you are carelessly leaving
your smudged blue fingerprints on the window sill.

Don't tell me that you are leaving
your warm impression in my bed
to grow cold in your absence.

Don't tell me.

So that I can wait
not knowing for certain if you'll come back.

So I can wait
to scrub your fingerprints from my skin.

So I can wait
to shake out the blankets.

Don't tell me.
So I can wait alone on Sunday morning
and hear my words echoed on the radio.

Weather Report

A cloud the color of wrinkled elephant hide
arose from your lips
heavy and sulfureous it

lifted ponderously from your open mouth
obscuring your eyes
but not its meaning

your words suspended darkly
condensing
as tears on my face

Heart Burn

Lit by sputtering flares of a candle
your photograph crumples
in the porcelain dish
like a dry autumn leaf

edges catch and curl
black ash spreads across your Sunday suit
splintering your ice blue stare
(How can your eyes be so cold?)

heat smudges your tight smile
thin and false
so much like it was when
you said good-bye.

You flamed into my life
smoldered too long
leaving behind the
burnt stench of betrayal.

Taste of Summer

Like sunscreen coating my nose and
saltwater sand scratching my bare toes the
taste of summer is sticky

like taffy stuck in my teeth
too-sugary lemonade that
puckers my cheeks

like pink cotton-candy tangled in my tousled hair
like watermelon juice dripping down my chin
black seeds stuck on sidewalk squares

sticky like memories of you
I can't let go

Finding You

"The art of losing isn't hard."
It's finding that confounds me.

Finding that referral for the new dentist
misplaced address to mail in the rebate
Emma's blue scarf I know I dropped ... somewhere
my keys my cell phone

where is that novel for book club?
If I could find time to read it.... or
one-dish recipes I cut from a magazine
to send my daughter?

Yet every morning with no exception
I find myself finding you in everything
your imprint etched forever
here in my heart.

Missing You

The back door stands open to
early morning drizzle
cool breezes slip through the screen
knock lightly against its weathered frame
soft rain shushes and hushes
like a clutch of whispering gossips

I am drawn closer by the
acrid tang of rain-speckled rust mingling
with the humid scrub of summer grass and
when I close my eyes the
damp wool of your red jacket
hung there so long ago

I pause

trying to recall the capitol of Lithuania
the brand of pesto I like
that movie idol from the 'fifties

I pause in the moon's shadow
to conjure up
all the lost facts I knew
last week or yesterday

I pause to consider
why they seem so important
when I am here with you
together in the dying light.

Salut

Walk with me
in the luminous glow of this sun-yellowed sky
Take my hand
on this dappled-green, apple green morning

until the eternal pull of earth claims you.

I wonder if you meant to leave your
        paint-smudged thumb prints for me to study?

If you intended to surrender the
        gentle breeze at the curtained window?

If you carelessly abandoned the
        warm blanket of comfort we wove?

I walk with you
under the quilt of the darkened sky
holding in my hand the
immeasurable loss of you.

Others

Advice to Writers

Don't think about
laundry lumped in the hamper or
mending lingering in the basket by the door.

Don't fret about
soup simmering on the stove or
chard waiting to be chopped for dinner.

Forget emails.
Ignore the bills.

It's Summer! Step outside
wriggle your grass-gentled toes in morning dew
allow your plans to sail away like kites on the wind

anticipate sun's nourishment
inhale all this green glorious light
into your soul.

Then drag your chair under the tallest shade tree
sketch a poem of bird song and a
prayer of gratitude for this
lush and luminous summer day.

What's in my journal?

hasty handwriting
unfinished sentences that leave me hanging
incomplete fragments that float off the page

subject/verb disagreements
like love/hurt
friendship/betrayal

secrets that can be shared
secrets that should be kept secret
inadmissible guilt

a desert of need
an ocean of want
a wave that covers all the rough sands of my heart
then retreats
leaving me smooth to write another day

Morning Jolt

I lurch wild-haired from my lair a
drooling dragon-lady trailing steaming droplets
from my treacherous jaws
whipping my scaly tail side to side
ROARING into the dawn.

Blame the alarm clock!

blasting me from my sweet eagle-dream of
lazily circling a cerulean sky
gliding on gently rising wind in the
cloudless warmth of morning
slipping quietly into daybreak.

Incomplete Sentencing

The evidence is clear
their verdict is in
a jury of peers concurs.
Guilty! they charge
of seeing this world differently

struggling juggling
my vision askew the
universe speaks
to me not you

inverting diverting
reverberating in me
echoing sounds and
colors only I can see.

So I stand accused
to this very day and
frankly would have it
no other way.

After A Long Day

empty out your pockets
brimming
with the flotsam of your day

take out the smooth slate pebble
shiny copper penny and
tangled piece of green string

pull out the paperback you thought you'd read
lint-crumpled grocery list and
flyer the young girl thrust into your hand

put it all on the table before you
this ordinary collection of artifacts
cataloguing another sacred day

Shhh

Words bubble to the surface of that
silent place in me
tempting stillness that lies on my tongue
insisting that
silence is not
emptiness

It is fertile
generative
trembling with promise
humming with electricity
filled with light breath memory
shimmering simmering
waiting

Pandemic Spring

After somber deaths and depths
of a year-long winter
Spring invites us to leave that all behind

beckons us to come outside
witness tender shoots poking through worn soil
trees pushing out tight pink buds.

My fingers fumble to unlatch the door
stuck shut with something that feels like fear
I struggle to push back into the world

haltingly hinges creak open
loosening hope held tightly in my
palm of despair.

Comeback

Listen. Turn
everything on
after a year of kneeling at the foot of the
Golden Mountain it's
time to flip the switch
crank up the volume
welcome the din
Shout
out
loud
vibrate with the cacophony of crowds
dance in the symphony of shared words.

Listen. Turn
full-on once more
towards the screeching, buzzing, roaring
extravagant noise of life.

Sonorous Clamor of Spring

I turned my back to the tumbling stream
on my creekside walk this morning
cupping my ears to magnify the bubble and gurgle
racing in 2/4 time over mossy stones
snagging on stubborn branches.

Gentle winds tried to nudge and ruffle new leaves
emerging from winter weary tree limbs
succeeding only in a whispered awakening.

Songbirds and reedy robins like
Divas in their feathered costumes
commanded the stage
piercing tones and tremulous trills
proclaiming that all the rest was only stage scenery
a minor- key backdrop for
their breathtaking arias.

Late Summer Picnic

Woodpeckers gathered here last night
nudging up against velvety green moss
nestling in among violets
warming themselves by the riverbank.

Undetected beneath the protective web of
broad umbrella leaves
they feasted on soft fragrant Mayapples
pecking a muted rat-a-tat tat-a-tat
heads bobbing in sweet synchronous rhythm.

Winter Wisdom

Magpie takes flight
freeing her claws from a crooked stile
cracking frigid silence with
a raspy screech
weaving with the wind gliding into
liminal space between cloud and snow.

I wonder if she meant to shatter
    this icy winter hush
carelessly trailing her snow shadow
    across the ground below
sensing my yearning to join her
    effortless climb through the starless night.

Earthbound I plod onward
heavy boots stenciling patterns in frozen slush
restless for the sheltering warmth of home
where beneath my worn woolen blanket
I slip into raven dreams soaring
untethered beyond earth's gravity.

The Music Lesson

Four white-washed convent walls
an open window
one bench
eighty-eight keys
ten fingers
il Prete Rosso and
me.

Riding a sunlit garden breeze the
Sonata tumbles out the window
falling lightly on playmates below.
They give chase
stumbling over elusive motifs
catching chords on open palms.

Holy Sisters in the habit of
witnessing miracles
held in the hands of angels
hear grace in every note.

A towering terracotta steeple
scraped by centuries of history
watches over ancient olive trees
giving shade to this garden of
sonorous music and laughter
joined together echoing
enduring traditions.

* il Prete Rosso (the Red Priest) is Antonio Vivaldi's nickname.

If Not The Sea

If not the sea
the idea of it
rolling echo of crashing waves
sting-of-salt air
foam snagged on sand like spun sugar
tiny creatures skittering back to murky depths.

If not the sea
the idea of
endless undulations
concealing the sultry siren of its allure
deep pull of the moon calling
tides whispering an invitation.

Why not the sea?

Amelia

She shields her eyes against late-summer sun
baking the Kansas wheat field
Flat
dense
fragrant as a yellow corn cake.
Earthbound she stands in seasonal stasis.

A murder of ink-black crows rises from the tall stalks
Caw!
Caw caw!
their wings sleek as tempered steel beat in unison
sharp-edged shape-shifters that climb and skitter
as they pull across the sky
each one calling her to reap
reckless delight in sky-bound flight.

Gratitude

The whole sky is mine
but I am willing to share

it's livelier with two of us
dancing in the wide open blue
holding hands
high-stepping through
puffy white clouds
swinging our arms in
rhythm with the wind.

This sky this dance an
extravagant privilege to share.

Fizzy

I can't hold gladness in my mouth for very long
nor would I want to

it slips out sliding down my chin like cold lemonade
shoots out in a wild spray of exuberance
rolls out loud and boisterous like
children tumbling down a hill.

My wide-mouthed jar of joy
lid off spilling over with delight.

Acknowledgements

This poetry collection is a result of the shared wisdom, humor and kindness of mentors Mary Hall Surface, Michelle Berberet, and Willona Sloan. They provide consistent guidance and opportunities for me to learn and grow as a writer. A heartfelt thank you for your support.

Thank you to my fellow writer, Rebecca, who poses the right questions to help shape my writing.

Merci beaucoup to Françoise for always listening and encouraging me to write more.

And, to the Salad group for motivating me to see what is still possible, many thanks.

About the Author

Raven is the pen name of Rose Avent, DC-based writer and poet currently living in Arlington, VA. Her poems have appeared in Georgetown University Lombardi Voices (2022, 2023, 2024). Rose was selected as a winner in the Moving Words Poetry contest (2022). Her winning poem was riding around on Buses in Arlington. She is an active member of Spellbinders, a national organization that promotes oral storytelling across generations.